(It's 1 sunshine and lollipops

Hayley Bryant

BookLeaf
Publishing

India | USA | UK

(It's not all) sunshine and lollipops © 2024
Hayley Bryant

Presentation by *BookLeaf Publishing*

Web: www.bookleafpub.com

E-mail: info@bookleafpub.com

ISBN: 9789358314687

First edition 2024

To my dad. My biggest supporter.

A reminder

Working myself up into a depression
Comes mostly from my insecurities
But who's rules are those I am working to
They're not mine, they're society's

Rather than focusing on my qualities
How lucky I am, what I do like
I dwell on what is lacking in me
Encouraging that deep darkness to strike

I write these poems of a reminder
To be thankful and be grateful
Ignore the outside judgements
We are all uniquely beautiful.

My body

I reprimand my body
For its conditions and ailments
It's failing me, stressing me
Sending my life into a derailment

I don't have the energy I should
Losing weight seems impossible
Aches, pains and pigmentation
Even though my tests are all 'optimal'

Without going on and on
Which would send me into a spiral
My body's failings seem unending
But they are far from final

There are many worse off
Some say I shouldn't complain
But my feelings are still valid
You don't understand my pain

What I will say is this
I want to change my outlook
To notice the parts of me I like
And write a more positive playbook

To the child in me

If I could wrap my arms around you, into a big
enveloping hug,
I don't think I'd ever let go. It's something we
both need so much.

While your life was never in danger, you would
have never come to harm,
The safety you craved was valid, to be loved and
never let down.

You are loved, exactly as you are, don't change a
single thing.
Embrace your strengths and flaws, reach out to
find your wings.

You're one of a kind, in the best possible way,
Go do great things, don't throw those dreams
away.

Dreams of love, adventure and happiness.
Whatever life throws at you, you'll get through
this.

Don't dim my glow!

Anxious brains breed anxious thoughts
Thoughts that ruminate and grow
Into detrimental thoughts, that
Take over and dim our glow.

Be the inspiration

Why are we always looking for approval
If someone else is doing that thing
Then it's ok, we're allowed to follow
As if we need permission to wear the bling

Be the inspiration you need
In your clothes, and especially your art
Your freedom will shine out from you
And you'll feel more complete deep in your
heart.

Adulting

Can we go back in time
To when life was just about fun
Away from obligations
And the pressure to go for a run

How are we suddenly adults
With responsibilities and such
Like parenting and mortgages
And all the bills that really suck

Now old enough to make decisions
And manage a team of five
But it's like it was just yesterday
That I was learning to drive.

Own your happiness

No-one owes you your happiness
Not your joy, your inspiration
Or your sorrow or your mess

Friends bring fun to our lives
But your boredom is your own
It's your responsibility to thrive

You are your number one priority
And your friends' are their own
It's your choice for mediocrity
And it's your choice alone!

When life is testing

When life is testing you
And you feel like giving up
Take a deep breath
And get some tasty grub

Ask yourself
What you need right now
To ease the stress and burden
And lift your heavy brow

This bad phase will pass
You'll still come out strong
It's the rollercoaster of life
But feeling down isn't wrong

The heaviness you feel
Is to help you pause
To reassess what's happening
And find a better cause

Though struggles in life are growth
With some valuable learnings
We still need to look after ourselves
And follow our inner yearnings.

Find your stillness

That thing that makes time stop still
Where the world around you is a blur
And you are completely present in that moment

That thing that makes you lose track of time
Forget to check your phone
You have everything you need right there

That thing that warms your heart
Lifts the edges of your lips unconsciously
Your thing, which brings you peace.

Living on my own

When I sit here in the silence
In the house I made a home
I smile because I'm not lonely
Though I'm very much alone

This peace is my sanctuary
From the rowdy outside bustle
I can be whoever I want to be
I'm not required to hustle

I made this space for me
I choose what goes on the walls
What music I play, food I eat
And who I let come through the doors

While I'd love to share this home
With someone I dearly love
I'll embrace this time I have
Rather than be dismissive of

There may come a time
Where I miss these days alone
With just my dog and tranquillity
In the house I made a home.

It isn't forever

Like a thick cloud all consuming
Not black and white but grey
Life hurries on around you
While you're so far away

No motivation or energy
But for necessary tasks
The cloud sucks out all your essence
Leaving you to wear a mask

Look out for the tiny speck
Of the colour coming through
It will gradually grow
And absorb back into you.

Single love

I love my little life
Yes, the one without a man
I don't have one at the moment
But if I really want one I can

I don't need a man to love my life
I am fulfilled a plenty
With fun and adventures
I am far from empty

My home is how I want it
I don't need to get permission
On how I paint or decorate
Whether the bed is in the right position

I have lots of love in my life
From friends, family and my dog
Romantic love would be nice
But I don't need him to be my rock

Being single has meant to me
I've learned to love myself
And find my joy and happiness
Without needing anyone else.

What they don't see

Like a clean and tidy house
With a cupboard full of crap
On the surface you're all fine
But underneath you're about to snap

The energy it takes
To keep that heaving cupboard closed
Drains you from your head
And right into your bones

The smile plastered on your face
Doesn't brighten up your eyes
It's only there for other people
So they don't see your silent cries

If you open up and tell them
You're not ok right now
They will surprise you
And even show you how

How friends will always be there
You're surely not a burden
Support from those around you
Is comforting and golden.

Single demon

Why do we demonise being single
As if there's something wrong with you
You're strong enough to be on your own
And not depend on anybody

Let's normalise being happy
Whether that's coupled up or alone
And celebrate achievements
Like finding a happiness of your own.

When I'm in a funk

When I'm in a funk
Or I'm feeling blue
Here are a few things to
Ask myself or do

How are you sitting?
Are you slumped?
With your shoulders
Round and humped

Do some yoga
Get outside
Take the dog along
For the ride

What do you need?
To make you number one
Take deep breaths
Til the darkness is gone.

The imposter

Who am I to advise
What wisdom do I have
I just a normal woman
With experiences that I've had

Who am I to teach
When I am still learning
My issues keep me stuck
While your world keeps turning

Who am I to coach
Someone out of a depression
While I'm also drowning
Searching for my own redemption

I am the ultimate imposter
Scrambling through life
Sharing how I get through
All the struggles and the strife.

My drop of sadness

You were there from the moment I was born
There, I thought you'd always be
To guide me through the journey of life
And be the biggest supporter of me

How do I carry on this journey
With this massive hole you've left
Missing your constant presence
And advice you've not given yet

I'm not the same person
I was when you were here
At first my life stood still
Engulfed with numbness and fear

I've gradually rebuilt
A new existence now
Where I can pick myself up
And be the one who stops me drown

Although I can see happiness
In my day and future too
I'll keep a drop of sadness
Sad, I'll always be missing you.

It's ok

It's ok if you feel down
And want to be alone
To feel solace in the peace
The space you call a home.

Sometimes solitude is needed
To sit with our feelings
Rather than let it build up
And then leave you reeling

It's ok to say no
To things you don't want to do
Or be cautious about doing something
Just because it's new

It's hard always being strong
We are allowed to falter
To find comfort in our own way
And combat the inner monster.

High functioning depression

I'm the one you never check on
Because I appear so strong
The one you don't worry about
Because there's never anything wrong.

On the outside I'm joyful
Make an effort and smile
I don't want to burden you
With what's going on inside.

I do what's necessary
Work and other commitments
They drain my energy so much
I have none left for fulfillments.

I'm there in body
And do what needs to be done
But my heart's not in it
I've lost all sense of fun.

It's not for forever
The grey clouds with fall away
All I ask is you check on me
In your own kind of way.

Go for it

Push yourself out of your comfort zone
Take risks
Trust that it will all work out

No-one ever regretted taking that chance
And the greats are not great by staying in their
lane.

Coping methods

I write to release my many thoughts
I play piano to block them out

I paint to quiet my mind
When meditation just won't do.

9 789358 314687